SOUTHERN EMUs BEFORE P............N

in Colour

For the Modeller and Historian

Bruce Oliver

Ian Allan

PUBLISHING

CONTENTS

Title page:
Penge West June 1983: '4VEP' No 7787 heads
an eight-coach semi-fast service from London
Bridge to Brighton, via Quarry. The bridge in
the background takes the down line from
Sydenham to Crystal Palace. A station at Penge
opened with the London & Croydon railway in
1839.

First published 2010

ISBN 978 0 7110 3470 9

Published by Ian Allan Publishing

an imprint of Ian Allan Publishing Ltd, Hersham,
Surrey, KT12 4RG
Printed in England by Ian Allan Printing Ltd,
Hersham, Surrey, KT12 4RG

Visit the Ian Allan Publishing website at
www.ianallanpublishing.com

INTRODUCTION

This is a sequel to the author's previous book, *British Railway Southern Region Electrics in Colour for the Modeller and Historian*, all photographs having been taken from the same archive. On this occasion, the focus is upon the 1970s and '80s, save for a few images from the 1960s and the 1990s. The evolution of 'Southern Electric' having already been covered in some depth in the earlier book, it is not intended here to reprise a detailed, historic chronology of the multiple-units featured, although the opportunity has been taken to effect some refinements and adjustments where appropriate. It is hoped the captions alone will suffice in the provision of unit details, where necessary. Reference is made, as a matter of course, to features other than the units themselves, embracing line history, architecture and infrastructure.

The period from 1970 to 1990 is largely remembered for the British Rail corporate identity of blue and grey, a somewhat severe image that affected the entire country. In 1970, it is true, there were still to be found Southern Region multiple-units in green livery although, by this time, they had become very much the worse for wear. By 1990, and in striking contrast to the British Rail corporate image, liveries representing sectorisation were appearing, offering welcome relief. On the Southern Region, it was the creation of Network SouthEast (NSE) in the mid-1980s that brought the greatest visual change. Nevertheless, it was to be many years before blue and grey finally vanished from the daily scene.

During the period under review, electric multiple-units (EMUs) could be found in five different liveries, excluding variations with yellow ends. These were, in summary, green, blue, blue and grey, 'Jaffa Cake', and NSE. The green of BR (SR) had virtually disappeared by the early 1970s, the new standard BR corporate identity having been introduced half a decade earlier, in the mid-1960s. The combination of blue and grey made a delayed entrance upon the Southern EMU scene yet, ironically, it had been seen on the Southern during the dying days of steam operation, as BR Standard locomotive-hauled rolling stock became repainted. It was thus surprising that new express rolling stock for the Bournemouth electrification scheme emerged in unrelieved Rail blue, exactly as applied to suburban units. However, following the launch of the blue and grey livery at Eastleigh in July 1967, the scene changed quickly during 1968, with Bournemouth main line rolling stock raised to the blue and grey national standard. The first

'4VEP' to be out-shopped in blue and grey was unit No 7808, considerably ahead of its classmates.

Suburban units continued to be painted in all-over Rail blue, including those of Southern Railway pedigree. It was not until the arrival of the Class 508s (1979-80) on the South Western Division that suburban rolling appeared in blue and grey. Subsequently, EPB rolling stock was out-shopped in blue and grey, during the period of refurbishment. Although main line Southern Railway 'COR' stock had been given the all-over Rail blue treatment from the mid-1960s, none was ever to appear in blue and grey. Also, '4SUB' rolling stock remained in all-over blue from repainting in the late 1960s through to withdrawal in the 1980s. It is of note that Class 508 stock was itself displaced in the early 1980s to join the Class 507 units on Merseyside, as Class 455 units entered service in 1982-85. Concurrent with these changes was the refurbishment programme of 'CEP' rolling stock, undertaken at Swindon Works from 1980, when six-digit identities were briefly carried.

When Network SouthEast was formed in the 1980s, a striking new livery was chosen, comprising bands of white, red and blue, with upward-angled features at driving cab ends. Initially, the shade of blue chosen was lighter than that settled upon in the years leading up to Privatisation, a decade later. The angle, carrying the lines up to the roof at cab ends, was, at the same time, modified to become a small radius arc. This livery was applied throughout the region, there being no distinguishing features between main line and suburban rolling stock – save for the introduction of short-lived 'route identities' on body sides. A brief interlude, providing remarkable contrast, had occurred within the South Eastern and Central divisions just prior to the formation of NSE. It took the form of an inspirational livery, appropriately nick-named 'Jaffa Cake', comprising bands of charcoal, orange and taupe, and could be found anywhere from Ramsgate to Portsmouth Harbour. It was unfortunate that the livery lasted only briefly, with relatively few units being so out-shopped, as it was most attractive.

During the period under review, Gatwick Express, created as a separate operation, introduced a livery based upon the InterCity swallow scheme of charcoal and taupe. Ten two-car and 19 three-car sets of Mk 2f locomotive-hauled rolling stock were formed into trains of different lengths, according to need, with Class 73 electro-diesel locomotives as motive power at the country end. At the

Waterloo April 1972: On the 8th of the month, with a farewell '5BEL' special, No 3053 waits to leave former platform 14 at 10.10. An ambitious itinerary took the special to Victoria, via Hounslow, Addlestone, Haslemere, Portsmouth Harbour, Barnham, Bognor Regis, Littlehampton, Christ's Hospital, Three Bridges, Eastbourne, Ore, Lewes, Seaford, Newhaven Harbour and Brighton. The non-stop journey from Brighton to Victoria took 55 minutes.

London end of these formations, former '2HAP' DMBSO vehicles converted for use as driving luggage vans (DMLVs) completed the arrangement for push-pull operation.

It was decided to extend electrification to Weymouth in the 1980s, thus dispensing with the Class 33/1 diesel-electric push-pull operation west of Bournemouth. With this development came the introduction to the Bournemouth main line of splendid new Mk 3 rolling stock, Class 442 (1988-89), usually referred to as 'Wessex' units. Twenty-four five-car units were built for the service. The transition did, nevertheless, impose a complicated period of change upon the division, as these new units were to be powered by 1967 electrical equipment recovered from '4REP' tractor units, then being displaced. During the change-over, remarkable variety displaced 21 years of uniformity on Bournemouth line services, involving ephemeral, hybrid formations, frequently combining with locomotives – invariably Class 73s, sometimes in pairs. Within a few years, the

Class 442s came to be shared between the Bournemouth and Portsmouth main lines, a practice that persisted well into the new century, almost a decade after Privatisation.

In the early 1990s, Network SouthEast's brain-child, the 'Networker', began to enter service on suburban lines in Kent, the four-car Class 465s (1991-94) and two-car Class 466s (1993-94). These units brought about the demise of EPB stock within the division. To eliminate EPB stock from the Central Division, a large batch of first-series Class 455 units (Nos 5801-5846) transferred from the South Western Division, augmented by 24 brand-new two-car Class 456 units (1990-91). The arrival of Class 365 (1994-95) express 'Networkers' in the South Eastern Division, heralded the withdrawal of 'CEP' rolling stock, as well as migration by some units to the South Western. In the previous decade, '4BEP' units, refurbished at Swindon, had displaced the 1970 '4BIG' units on Portsmouth services, the latter batch of buffet units transferring to the Central Division.

In the quarter century from 1970 to Privatisation, there had, in fact, been an uninterrupted process of change, embracing reallocation of units, refurbishment, renumbering schemes, reformations, new liveries, new deliveries and, of course, withdrawals. It can scarcely be the task of this book, given the space available, to address the mountain of historical minutiae that span the period under review. Rather, the purpose here is to record scenes in colour of electric multiple units as seen in service, in the context of the time, featuring buildings and infrastructure, as

well as the units themselves. As no photograph here has previously appeared in a book, it is hoped the collection will contribute usefully to the archive of material on the subject. If, by chance, any individual photograph manages to fulfil a particular need or answer a specific question, so much the better.

Knowing that it would be impossible to satisfy all tastes in the choice of picture order, thought was given to the possibilities, viz. date, classes of units, operating divisions line order and location. For many reasons, not least the fact that no index is provided, location in alphabetical order has been chosen; this avoids several potential problems, whilst establishing a recognisable plan. Given the title of the book, the settings in which trains are to be found are as important as the trains themselves. Pictures have been assembled under three distinct headings; the central body of representative material is flanked by an introductory review of pre-World War 2 Southern Railway survivors, while a brief reference to the newer, third-generation units, brings the period under review to a close. In the latter case, reference is necessarily brief, bearing in mind these units are to feature in a separate title, given the crucial role they have played since Privatisation.

Bruce Oliver
Southsea
2010

SOUTHERN RAILWAY PRE WORLD WAR 2 ROLLING STOCK

Right:
Ascot August 1971: '4COR' No 3135 enters on a service from Reading, travelling via Brentford to Waterloo. Ascot is one of several Southern stations with a platform face either side of a single running line. The line from Staines had reached Ascot in June 1856. The '4COR' units ended their working lives on both these and 'Coastway' services.

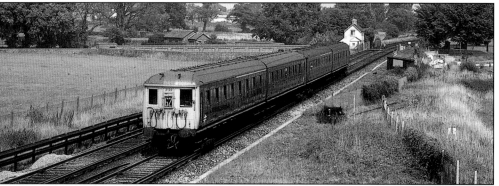

Left:
Bedhampton August 1970: Having just left the station, No 2139 and another '2BIL' unit head for Portsmouth Harbour on a stopping service from Brighton. Rusting track, just visible by the leading unit, once served the adjacent water works.

Below:
Brighton August 1968: '4LAV' No 2949 stands at the buffers to Platform 6, beneath the grand train shed, erected in 1882/3. Blue BRUTE baggage trolleys, a creation of the 1960s, litter the platforms.

Above:

Brighton April 1972: '4COR' units spent their final months on 'Coastway' routes. No 3122 enters Platform 2, having come from Portsmouth Harbour on a semi-fast service (Code 60). The site of the former motive power depot is in the centre of the picture, since put to alternative use. Another '4COR', No 3163, one of the hybrid series (Nos 3159-3168), occupies the carriage sidings alongside Platform 1, while a Class 73 electro-diesel ('ED') rests in a siding to the right.

Below:

Brighton April 1972: '5BEL' No 3051 waits in Platform 4, forming a return non-stop service to Victoria. The train shed ironwork had recently been repainted in a brown and red colour scheme. Sadly, the all-Pullman '5BEL' units did not escape the corporate image diktat from on high, indiscretion scarcely ever having been taken to such lengths to make a point.

Below:

Brighton April 1972: The eastern approach to the station, with the former works now just a memory. The site subsequently became a car park. '4COR' No 3123 enters Platform 9 on a stopping service from Ore. The '4COR' units had just a few weeks to go.

Bottom:

Camberley August 1971: The station is seen largely as it was when opened in 1878 as 'Camberley and York Town'. '4COR' No 3141 stops for business, while operating between Aldershot and Waterloo. Telegraph poles were once very much a feature of the railway scene, their robust presence and associated wires often being a source of inconvenience for photographers.

Left:
Chichester September 1971: '4COR' No 3149 leaves the station, bound for Brighton on a stopping service from Portsmouth Harbour.

Below:
Fratton August 1970: Repainted in Rail blue is instruction unit No S10, renumbered 053 in 1971. It had been created as '3SUB' No 1782, in about 1929/30, from ex-LSWR loco-hauled stock. Seen here parked alongside the EMU depot, it was withdrawn in 1974.

Left:
Frimley August 1971: The section between Frimley and Ash Vale Junction is single track, providing an interesting setting for '4COR' No 3130, as it travels towards Aldershot, where it will reverse for the onward journey to Guildford.

Right:
Hilsea September 1971: During their last few months, '4COR' units were used on services operating out of Brighton, east and west along the coast, embracing Ore and Portsmouth Harbour. Unit No 3155 is seen between Hilsea and Fratton on a stopping service to Portsmouth Harbour.

Below:
Liss July 1968: The station, rich in historical features, receives '4COR' No 3106, racing along on a fast service to Waterloo from Portsmouth Harbour. The period signalbox is joined by other railway buildings, barley-twist, swan-neck gas lamps, and period platform seating, to complete a time-capsule – with roses in full bloom embellishing the scene. Only the three-aspect colour light signal announces that time is moving on – soon to claim No 3106 as a victim of progress.

Above:
Margate October 1972: The '4COR' valedictory tour took in main lines in Kent. No 3143, with No 3102 behind, finds itself at Margate, where the Southern Railway station building of 1926 expresses the solid confidence of the early days after the Grouping. The Southern Railway very quickly redrew the railway map of Thanet completely, bringing great benefit.

Below:
Patcham November 1964: '6PUL' No 3006 approaches the northern entrance to the 492-yard tunnel, with a service from Victoria to Littlehampton. This setting has since been transformed almost beyond recognition with the completion of the A27 Brighton bypass.

Above:

Portcreek Junction February 1970: A meeting of three liveries near the junction, as a Waterloo stopping service, comprising a pair of '2BIL' units, passes a '4CEP' unit, on a train from Victoria to Portsmouth Harbour. The land within the Cosham triangle has since become an industrial estate, but the former railway properties survive in residential use.

Right:

Rowlands Castle August 1970: Doyen '4COR' unit No 3101 rounds the station curve with a Waterloo to Portsmouth Harbour train, only a few weeks before the class was finally eliminated from the route, with the arrival of the new '4CIG/BIG' units. The station dates from the 1859 line opening.

Above:

Seaford August 1968: A collection of pre-World War 2 rolling stock meets by the station, the '2HAL' unit under the canopy providing the service. The final '2BIL' unit, No 2152, is parked in the bay platform, while a '4COR', a '4BUF' (No 3083) and another '2BIL' occupy the siding. The line containing the '2HAL' survives, with Seaford now a long siding from Newhaven. The line from Newhaven to Seaford opened in 1864, 17 years after that connecting Lewes with Newhaven.

Below:

Walton-on-Thames June 1971: A 12-coach '4COR' rake, led by No 3159, passes through, pounding the track on a peak-period service to Farnham. With the delivery of '4CIG' units reaching completion, the days of the '4CORs' on these services were, by this time, numbered.

SUCCESSORS TO SOUTHERN RAILWAY PRE WORLD WAR 2 ROLLING STOCK INCLUDING CLASSES 508 AND 455

Above:
Addiscombe June 1976: The EMU depot is seen from the station platform, with the signalbox and semaphores completing the scene. The line from Elmers End to Sanderstead was later closed, to be superseded, in part, by the Croydon tram scheme.

Below:
Adisham May 1985: The original station buildings of 1861 survive, although the goods shed was, by this time, already in alternative use. An eight-coach 'VEP' formation leaves the station, on its way to Dover Priory from Victoria, with No 7762 leading.

Above:
Amberley May 1982: Seen from above the north portal to the 83-yard North Stoke Tunnel is '4CIG' No 7336, the last member of the Phase I batch, heading an eight-coach stopping service away from the station, en route from Victoria to Bognor Regis. The line from Dorking to Arundel Junction was electrified in 1938.

Centre left:
Amberley May 1982: The northern approach to the station, with '4VEP' No 7803 on a stopping service from Victoria to Bognor Regis. Amberley station opened with the line from Hardham Junction to Ford in 1863, Pulborough to Petworth having pre-dated this development by four years, in 1859.

Left:
Amberley August 1983: The signal frame is stowed away beneath the canopy on the down platform. In this scene, '4CIG' No 7380 is found on a stopping service from Victoria to Bognor Regis.

Left:

Arundel August 1981: '4CIG' No 7373 arrives with a Bognor Regis to Victoria stopping service. The goods shed is no longer rail connected, but survives in alterative use. Arundel had opened as 'New Arundel' in August 1863. A separate covered area, from a much later date, is seen on the down platform, with the Southern Railway signalbox beyond.

Bottom left:

Ashford June 1982: Taken from the former down island platform, now dedicated to Eurostar services, '4CEP' No 411601, carrying the briefly fashionable six-digit identification, rushes by on a boat train from Victoria to Dover. '4VEP'
No 7760 stands in the platform on a service from Charing Cross to Margate.

Right:

Ashford June 1982: A 12-coach boat train uses the up through line, with '4CEP' No 7187 leading, bound for Victoria, via Herne Hill, having come from Dover. A '4VEP' stands at the down main platform, later rebuilt for exclusive use by Eurostar services, when the station was renamed Ashford International.

Below:

Ashtead June 1986: Refreshed '4EPB' No 5436 leaves on a Victoria to Horsham service. The station opened in 1859, although the present structure is a total rebuild, lacking any detectable architectural merit. The line through Ashtead was electrified with the 1925 South Western Division scheme from Raynes Park to

Left:
Aylsham May 1985: '4CEP' No 1562 leads an eight-coach Dover Priory-Victoria train through the station, one modernised in an aesthetically minimalist style. The station opened in 1928, in response to developments in the Kent coalfield.

Below:
Balcombe August 1977: '4CIG' No 7434 emerges from the tunnel-like overbridge, working a Victoria service from Ore, Hastings and Eastbourne. Balcombe station opened in 1841. Simple canopies and ironwork provide sufficient cover for waiting passengers.

Right:
Balcombe Tunnel Junction August 1977: Prior to track rationalisation, a 12-coach train from Ore, Hastings and Eastbourne takes the fast line to Three Bridges, en route to Victoria with '4CIG' No 7387 at the head.

Bottom right:
Balcombe Tunnel Junction May 1978: '4CIG' No 7433 leads a 12-coach semi-fast train to Brighton via the Quarry line towards the junction. Upon remodelling, the pointwork was moved further north, towards Three Bridges.

Left:

Battledown August 1988: A semi-fast service from Waterloo to Bournemouth passes the point where the Exeter line diverges. Two '4CIG' units feature, No 1264 in BR blue/grey, the other in the then recently introduced NSE scheme. The 12xx series was an intermediate numbering scheme, between the original 73xx/74xx series and the final TOPS 18xx scheme.

Right:

Beckenham Junction August 1979: The southern bay platform has '4SUB' No 4710 in occupation, waiting to return to Victoria, via Crystal Palace. This was one the Class 405s later fitted with roller blind route boxes. The north side bay platform is visible beyond the canopy, with a siding beyond that – here containing wagons, but freight traffic is no more. Croydon Tramlink now extends to the south side of the station, having taken over the former up line as far Birkbeck Junction.

Below:

Bedhampton May 1982: In this scene, the crossing is controlled by a tidy signalbox – since superseded by CCTV. '4VEP' No 7844 forms a stopping service from Waterloo to Portsmouth & Southsea. The station opened in 1906.

Above:
Bickley March 1982: '4CEP' No 1530 passes through on a service from Dover Priory to Victoria, via Canterbury East. Bickley had been approached from both directions when the railway was built, the line from Bromley arriving in 1858, that from Rochester coming two years later, in 1860.

Below:
Bickley March 1982: The approach to the station from Bromley South hits an adverse 1-in-95 gradient. '4EPB' No 5213 is arriving at the station on a stopping service to Sevenoaks, via Bat & Ball. The unit to the right is parked in a siding, since lifted.

Left:
Bickley March 1982: Looking towards Bickley Junction from beneath the road overbridge, '2HAP' No 6116 heads a four-coach formation that has come from Sevenoaks, via Bat & Ball.

Bottom left:
Birchington-on-Sea May 1986: '4CEP' No 1547, disgracefully dirty up front, calls on a service from Victoria to Ramsgate. The station dates from 1863, when the line was extended from Herne Bay to Ramsgate Harbour. Electrification arrived as part of the Phase I scheme of 1959.

Right:
Bognor Regis September 1982: '4VEP' No 7724 is about to arrive at the terminus station with a stopping train from Victoria. The signalbox is on the up side of the line, just a few yards to the south at this point.

Below:
Bognor Regis February 1984: The signalbox is of Southern Railway design. In the distance are the carriage storage sidings situated alongside the terminus station of 1902. The first station on this site, dating from 1864, had been destroyed by fire in 1899. However, the original 'Bognor' station had been at Woodgate, and was opened in 1846. '4CIG' No 7435 leaves the station on a stopping service to Victoria via Littlehampton.

Right:

Bookham June 1986: Opened in 1885 as the only station on the line between Leatherhead and Effingham Junction, Bookham was contemporary with the 'New Line' to Guildford from Hampton Court Junction. Class 455 No 5709 heads a train from Waterloo towards Effingham Junction. This is a member of the second batch of such units, using one trailer coach per unit from Class 508 stock, made redundant when these units were transferred to Merseyside services in the mid-1980s as three-coach units.

Below:

Borough Green & Wrotham May 1985: Substantial LCDR architecture and canopies grace the down side platform, probably dating from the opening of the line from Otford Junction to Maidstone in 1874. '4VEP' No 7771, leading another of its class, is operating a Victoria to Margate service, via Canterbury West.

Right:

Bosham April 1984: The station, dating from the opening of the line to Portsmouth in 1847, receives '4VEP' No 7733, working a stopping service from Brighton to Portsmouth Harbour. The original shelter on the up platform has since been replaced by a modern structure, while the down side buildings remain unaltered.

Left:

Bosham August 1987: Phase I '4CIG' No 1726 passes the then recently repainted signalbox, while working a Portsmouth Harbour to Victoria service. The box has since been demolished.

Below:

Bramshott April 1988: A Class 73 powers a mixed formation near milepost 36, on a fast service from Bournemouth to Waterloo, during the months when the '4REP' units were being disbanded. The leading three vehicles, buffet included, are the remnants of a 'REP', coupled ahead of a pair of 'TC' sets.

Above left:
Brighton August 1979: Originally the station had 10 platforms, provision being reduced, in stages, to eight. The trackbed of Platform 10 is seen to the right in this view, as '2HAP' No 6058 enters Platform 9 on a service from Eastbourne.

Left:
Brighton April 1980: The site of the former Brighton Works has since seen alternative use as a car park. '4BEP' No 7002 arrives at the head of a train from Victoria. London Road Viaduct, carrying the line to Lewes, provides an architectural backdrop of great distinction, while the signalbox still bears a Southern Railway enamel sign, announcing Brighton. No 7002 was one of the original pair of '4BEP' units, entering service several years prior to the production series.

Above:
Brighton April 1980: '4CIG' No 7368 brings a 12-coach train past Lovers Walk EMU depot, on a fast service to Victoria.

Below:
Burgess Hill August 1979: The station witnesses the departure of a Victoria to Littlehampton service, with '4BIG' No 7032 in charge. Burgess Hill opened in 1841, with the main line to Brighton.

Above:

Canterbury East May 1985: With the elevated signalbox and former goods shed in view, an eight-coach '4VEP' formation departs on a service from Victoria to Dover Priory. Unit No 7761 leads the way. Faversham to Canterbury had opened in 1860, the continuation to Dover Town following almost exactly a year later.

Below:

Caterham October 1975: '2EPB' No 5666 rests at the buffers to Platform 1 at the branch terminus. Opened in 1856, services from Charing Cross were electrified in 1928.

Right:

Chartham May 1985: '4CEP' No 1530 passes the neat signalbox, en route from Margate to Victoria, via Maidstone East and Herne Hill. The station was opened in 1859, 13 years after the line itself linking Ashford and Canterbury.

Below right:

Chatham May 1976: Emerging from the 297-yard Chatham Tunnel is '2HAP' No 6144, leading a train from Margate to Victoria, via Herne Hill. The station opened with the line to Faversham in January 1858, while the line to the west opened just two months later.

Top right:
Chichester April 1982: '4BIG' No 7051 fronts an eight-coach formation on a Portsmouth Harbour to Victoria service. It is seen coming past lines of sidings in use by the engineering department. Subsequently, the sidings fell into desuetude but have, more recently, been reinstated for the stockpiling of aggregates.

Centre right:
Chichester April 1988: '4CIG' No 1263 gathers speed en route to Portsmouth Harbour, having come from Victoria. The view of the yard demonstrates its use at the time, by the engineering department. The unit is here identified in the intermediate 12xx numbering scheme.

Below:
Chichester April 1982: '4VEP' No 7787 charges away, forming a stopping train to Portsmouth Harbour from Brighton.

Above:
Christ's Hospital September 1975: The signalbox and semaphore stand in the 'V' of a former junction. Here, the branch line to Guildford left the main line to Arundel Junction, to which latter point '4VEP' No 7722 is heading.

Below:
Clapham Junction March 1977: A diverted South Eastern Division service passes Clapham Junction 'B' signalbox on the approach to Platform 15. '4VEP' No 7889 leads the 12-car formation.

Left:
Clapham Junction May 1982: '4VEP' No 7820 arrives in Platform 9, forming a 'New Line' (via Cobham) service to Guildford. '4VEP' units revived the use of first class accommodation on the route, a choice denied to passengers when Class 455s took over Cobham line diagrams, not long afterwards.

Below:
Clapham Junction May 1983: '4VEP' No 7845 arrives in Platform 6 with a service from Waterloo to Windsor & Eton Riverside. In the left background the line from Ludgate GW Junction to Latchmere No 2 Junction can just be glimpsed.

Right:
Clapham Junction December 1983: Class 455 No 5828 enters Platform 4, on a cold, misty morning. Clapham Junction 'C' signalbox occupies the space between the lines, at the country end of the island structure forming Platforms 3 and 4. This box survived for many years in a very dilapidated condition but has since been demolished.

Below right:
Clapham Junction March 1984: The land between sections 'A' and 'B' at Clapham Yard hosts a line of Class 455 units, with No 5860 up front. The experimental 1970s '4PEP' unit, the prototype for Class 508, is seen parked out of the way to the left.

Right:

Clayton Tunnel August 1977: The north portal of the 1 mile 499 yard tunnel is architecturally flamboyant, a folly of some distinction. The property positioned over the tunnel mouth is inhabited, where there can never be a dull moment. Here, a '4VEP' emerges into the daylight with a service from Littlehampton to Victoria.

Below:

Cosham June 1995: '4CIG' No 1317, a 'Greyhound' variation, arrives on a service from Portsmouth & Southsea to Waterloo. Driving vehicles were painted black above the gangway and unit numbers, not long before Privatisation, allegedly to camouflage accumulated dirt.

Left:

Coulsdon North April 1983: A bleak scene, shortly before closure, with Bulleid-profile '2EPB' No 5678 waiting to leave on a Victoria service via Selhurst. Coulsdon North opened as 'Stoats Nest' in 1899.

Right:

Coulsdon North April 1983: With the station to the left, '4CIG' No 7394 fronts a 12-coach train to Eastbourne, Hastings and Ore, via the Quarry line. The platforms on the fast lines were out of use by this time. The '2EPB' on the left is returning from the Tattenham Corner branch, while the unit on the right takes the original main line route, via Redhill. Coulsdon North was, in 1925, one of the last sections to be electrified by the overhead system, converting to third rail in 1929.

Below:

Dartford May 1976: '4EPB' No 5148 forms the rear unit of a (Charing Cross or Cannon Street) train at Platform 3. Dartford was first served by the railway in 1849 with the coming of the North Kent Railway. The original buildings do not survive, the station having succumbed to modernisation during a period when inspirational architecture was not on the agenda.

Above left:
Denmark Hill March 1982: The 132-yard Grove Tunnel stands at the east end of the station. '4VEP' No 7868 is seen coming west, en route to Victoria with a train from Margate, via Ashford and Maidstone East.

Left:
Denmark Hill March 1982: '4CEP' No 1580 passes through the station, having just emerged from Grove Tunnel, leading a Dover to Victoria service via Canterbury East and Catford. The elaborate Italianate architectural features that define this station are here seen above the A215 road bridge. A serious fire occurred in 1980, damaging the building; it was subsequently restored. The LCDR and LBSCR had opened for business here in 1865 and 1866, respectively.

Above:
Dover August 1979: '4VEP' No 7854 emerges from the distinctive portals of the1,387-yard Shakespeare Tunnel, at the head of a service from Charing Cross to Margate, via Dover. This geologically difficult section of track dates from 1844.

Below:
Dover April 1984: An eight-car formation, comprising two '4VEP' units, with No 7865 leading, skirts the coast on the approach to Shakespeare Tunnel, en route from Margate to Charing Cross. The erstwhile goods yard in the background, to the right of the Lord Warden hotel, occupied the site of the former steam motive power depot.

Above:
Dover August 1974: '4CEP' No 7126 emerges from the 158-yard Priory Tunnel to enter Priory station on a service from Margate to Charing Cross. Semaphore signalling and an immaculate signalbox complete the period scene.

Below:
Dover August 1974: Priory station finds '2HAP' No 6112 and '4CEP' No 7157 in Platforms 3 and 1, respectively, the '4CEP' having arrived from Victoria via Faversham. Dover Priory station had been opened by the LCDR in 1861, but was subsequently rebuilt.

Left:
Dumpton Park May 1986: Opened by the Southern Railway in 1926, this station was part of a major programme of reconstruction. After the line to Ramsgate Harbour closed, trains turned right at the point of descent to the tunnel, to make for the present Ramsgate station. '4CEP' No 1566 is operating a stopping service to Victoria from Ramsgate via Margate.

Below:
Earlswood April 1984: '4CIG' No 7315 rounds the bend at high speed, on a Victoria-Gatwick Airport shuttle in place of a '4VEG' unit. There were 12 '4VEPs' converted with additional luggage accommodation for this service ('Vestibule Electro Gatwick') but they invariably wandered away from their prescribed duties, leaving the service to anything else available. In the background, the line on the left leads to Redhill, while that to the right is the Quarry Line cut-off of 1899/1900.

Right:
Eastleigh April 1985: '4TC' (unpowered 'Trailer Control') set No 426 is at the head of a 12-coach formation on a Waterloo to Weymouth service. This set would have continued to Weymouth, hauled by a Class 33/1 diesel-electric locomotive, leaving the other 'TC' set and the motorised '4REP' unit at Bournemouth.

Bottom right
Eastleigh June 1985: A special completes the depot loop with preserved units '2BIL' No 2090 and '4SUB' No 4732 providing the rolling stock.

Above:
East Croydon July 1988: Class 455 No 5830 negotiates the cutting south of the station, on a service from Caterham to London Bridge.

Right:
East Croydon March 1983: Phase I '4CIG' No 7328 enters platform 3 on a non-stop 'Gatwick Express' service from Victoria. A batch of '4VEP' units had been modified as '4VEG', specifically for Gatwick services but non-dedicated rolling stock frequently deputised. In this view towering cranes are at work on buildings that transformed the local skyline.

Below:
Eastbourne August 1979: A 12-coach rake of 'CIG/BIG' stock arrives from Victoria, where unit No 7357 will end its journey. One or two of the remaining two units will reverse here for the onward journey to Hastings and Ore. A commanding signalbox oversees operations, with semaphore signals controlling movements.

Left:

Effingham Junction July 1980: '4SUB' No 4658 leads a two-unit train bound for Waterloo via Epsom. It will have reversed in the siding beyond the carriage shed, seen to the left of the picture, partially obscured by trees. Effingham Junction station opened in 1888 on the 'New Line' to Guildford via Cobham, the line itself having opened in 1885. Waiting shelters are provided on each platform but the ticket office is at road level, by an overbridge at the London end.

Bottom left:

Effingham Junction December 1982: '4VEP' No 7738 pauses on a Guildford service from Waterloo via Cobham. With the arrival of the Class 455s on these services shortly afterwards, first class accommodation was removed from regular 'New Line' diagrams.

Right:

Effingham Junction July 1980: With the sub-station in the background, '4SUB' No 4696 rounds the corner from Leatherhead, its journey from Victoria via Mitcham Junction about to terminate. The line joined is that connecting Guildford and Cobham.

Below:

Elmers End August 1979: '2EPB' No 5744 waits to leave on a branch service to Addiscombe, the trackbed of which line is now largely incorporated in the Croydon tram system. The line to Addiscombe opened in 1864, the branch to Hayes following 18 years later, in 1882.

Above:
Elmstead Woods March 1982: '4EPB' No 5151 enters Platform 4 on a stopping service from Charing Cross to Orpington. It has just emerged from the 649-yard Chislehurst Slow Tunnel on a section of line opened to Chislehurst in 1865. In 1988, a batch of 32 '4EPBs' was re-formed to incorporate two compartment trailers. Numbered 5501-32, they were restricted to peak period operation.

Below:
Farnborough May 1967: '4TC' No 411, together with another trailer set of this class, is being propelled by 'ED' No E6027, on a fast service to Bournemouth. The location is near to the summit at milepost 31, 2½ miles east of Farnborough Main.

Left:

Farnborough August 1983: Near to the summit at milepost 31, a 12-coach rake of 'REP/TC' stock heads for Waterloo, with unit No 3005 providing the motive power. The train is a semi-fast service from Bournemouth.

Centre left:

Farnham August 1988: The country end of the station has a neat signalbox positioned where evidence of a crossing survives. '4VEP' No 3077, numbered in the intermediate TOPS scheme, leaves the station to continue its journey to Alton. Farnham was initially rail-connected from Guildford via Tongham in 1849, the line continuing to Alton in 1852. The direct line to Brookwood came much later, in 1870 and electrification arrived in 1937.

Below:

Fishbourne August 1987: The signalbox stood at the junction for the Midhurst branch and controlled the former A27 road crossing at this point. '4VEP' No 3095 passes the box on a stopping service from Portsmouth Harbour to Brighton. The unit number is in the intermediate TOPS series for Class 423, an interlude between the original numbering (77xx series) and the final series (34xx), following mid-term refurbishment.

Above left:

Fishbourne April 1987: '4VEP' No 3080 passes over the former A27 road crossing at the approach to Chichester, with a stopping service from Portsmouth Harbour to Brighton.

Left:

Fleet August 1983: An intimate scene, as '4VEP' No 7707, a member of the initial batch, enters the station to do business on a stopping train to Bournemouth. Fleet station had been rebuilt in 1966 in the undistinguished Clasp style of 'architecture', at a time when electrification of the route to Bournemouth was well advanced.

Top:

Folkestone Warren April 1984: An eight-coach boat train from Dover to Victoria via Herne Hill, formed of two refurbished '4CEP' units, traces its way along the coastal route, and is seen here approaching Martello Tunnel with No 1573 leading the way.

Right:

Forest Hill June 1983: Refreshed '4EPB' No 5436 arrives with a train for Caterham. The station had been rebuilt, the original having dated from the line's opening in 1839, when it carried the name 'Dartmouth Arms'.

Above:
Forest Hill June 1983: '4CAP' No 3208 races along, heading for London Bridge, having come from Reigate and Redhill. The '4CAP' units comprised pairs of former '2HAPs' coupled in semi-permanent union. 32xx and 33xx units represented '2HAP' Phases I and II, respectively.

Below:
Fratton August 1981: '4BIG' No 7049 leads an eight-coach train on a service from Portsmouth Harbour to Victoria. This unit, at the time allocated to the Central Division, had started life in 1970, operating between Portsmouth Harbour and Waterloo on the 1859 Direct line.

Above:

Fratton May 1984: Former '2HAL' units Nos 2624 and 2642 each contributed a vehicle to departmental stores unit No 023, here awaiting disposal following withdrawal. The unit is parked in a siding alongside the erstwhile goods shed.

Left:

Fulwell Junction September 1986: The lines from Kingston and Twickenham meet near Strawberry Hill depot, for the branch to Shepperton. In this view, lines of withdrawn '2HAP' units await their fate at the depot, while Class 455 No 5836 proceeds to Shepperton on a train from Waterloo via Kingston. Strawberry Hill had been a suburban steam motive power depot until superseded by Feltham, as local services became electrified. The Shepperton branch had been built by the Thames Valley Railway, the original intention having been continuation to reach Chertsey.

Above:

Gillingham August 1979: Activity on the down platform, where '4CEP' No 7115 is about to leave on its journey to Ramsgate, having come from Victoria via Herne Hill. When the line was opened from Chatham in 1858, this station was known as 'New Brompton'. Electrification reached Gillingham just prior to World War 2, when '2HAL' units were introduced. In this view, '2EPB' No 5734 is parked on the other side of the up platform.

Left:

Goring-by-Sea February 1984: The signalbox is being passed by '4CIG' No 7380, working from Littlehampton to Brighton.

Below:

Gravesend May 1976: The station served as the starting point for steam services to Grain, a branch that was never electrified. On the main line, electric trains reached Gravesend from Dartford in July 1930, with the eastern extension of the system to Maidstone West and Gillingham coming nine years later, just prior to World War 2. '4EPB' No 5244 is entering the up platform with a terminating service from Charing Cross.

SOUTHERN EMUs BEFORE PRIVATISATION

Above:

Grove Park August 1979: The short branch to Bromley North leaves the former SER main line from this station and dates from 1878. A branch shuttle service is seen leaving Platform 1, on a line that connects with the up fast, just to the north of the station. The unit is '2EPB' No 5707, an early member of the class. The raised concrete panel, right, had previously carried a Southern Railway enamel sign.

Below:

Guildford July 1983: '4VEP' No 7755 has just come through the 845-yard Chalk Tunnel on a service from Portsmouth Harbour to Waterloo. Nos 7755 and 7756 were the two '4VEP' units in which original windows with ventilators (subsequently sealed) were replaced by plain glass.

Above left:

Hampton Court August 1979: The station opened in 1849 and the line was electrified in 1916. '4SUB' No 4670 waits at the island platform on a Waterloo service. Evidence of a more extensive layout survives in this view, since reduced further to a pair of lines.

Left:

Hastings April 1985: '4BIG' No 7039 leaves with a service to Victoria, via Eastbourne, where another four-coach unit will be attached. In the station, a Hastings diesel-electric multiple unit (DEMU) is seen in Platform 4, on the left, while a two-coach diesel unit occupies Platform 1, on the right, with a service to Ashford.

Top:

Hastings April 1985: '4BIG' No 7036 enters the station, having recently started its journey at Ore. En route to Victoria, it will reverse in Eastbourne, the train strengthened with a further unit.

Right:

Havant August 1991: '4VEP' No 3095 with an eight-coach semi-fast train from Waterloo to Portsmouth Harbour, is seen leaving the station, which was completely transformed immediately following the 1937 electrification, when through lines were installed. By the time this picture was taken, the up through line had already been removed. More recently, the down through line has also disappeared, but, with the latest signalling scheme, both platform lines have become bi-directional, with accompanying pointwork.

Above:
Havant February 1989: Phase II '4CIG' No 1249 leads a semi-fast service from Portsmouth Harbour to Waterloo past the imposing signalbox. The branch line to Hayling Island, which closed in 1963, took a path on the other side of the box. The former goods yard occupied land on the north side of the station, where vehicles are seen parked.

Below:
Hayes August 1979: The branch terminus has '4EPB' No 5243 waiting to leave, bound for Cannon Street via Lewisham. Hayes joined the railway map in 1882, but the present buildings date from Southern Railway rebuilding. A double-sided platform survives, the storage siding having since been removed. The station suffered bomb damage during World War 2.

Above:
Herne Bay May 1985: An eight-coach '4CEP' formation departs with unit No 1550 leading. Herne Bay opened in 1861. A substantial station building survives on the down side but the up side island platform outer face is now out of use.

Right:
Hilsea March 1995: Nearing the station, which opened during World War 2, is Phase I '4CIG' No 1736, operating a Portsmouth Harbour to Brighton stopping train. In NSE livery, the unit displays the later fashion, a black-painted roof line above the gangway, allegedly to camouflage dirt.

Below:
Holborn Viaduct August 1979: An appropriately bleak scene is provided by the reduced layout at this terminus on a wet August afternoon. '4EPB' No 5036 awaits departure on a service to West Croydon. Holborn Viaduct station closed in 1990 with the reopening of the route to north London, via Snow Hill Tunnel.

Above left:
Horsham July 1981: With its solid concrete structures the station announces Southern Railway modernism. '4CIG' No 7334 is in Platform 3 on a Victoria to Portsmouth service, while '4SUB' No 4674 has recently arrived on a service from Waterloo.

Left:
Hove April 1980: The Cliftonville spur permits trains to travel from Preston Park towards Worthing, avoiding Brighton. '4CIG' No 7405 heads a 12-coach Littlehampton train round the corner into Hove, with the 535-yard Cliftonville Tunnel in view. The spur dates from 1879 and was electrified 53 years later.

Above:
Holland Road April 1980: Near the site of Holland Road Halt, opened in 1905, '4VEP' No 7757 travels the last few yards from Hove to Brighton, on a semi-fast service from Portsmouth Harbour.

Below:
Horley April 1984: A Gatwick Express service powered by 'ED' No 73123, is almost at the end of its brief journey from London. No 73123, here carrying the name *Gatwick Express*, began life as No E6030. Later renumbered 73206, it eventually passed to GB Railfreight, acquiring the name *Lisa*.

Above:
Hove April 1985: On a day when Brighton was closed for passengers, services used Hove as a temporary terminus. '4VEP' No 7798 waits to leave Platform 1 on a semi-fast service to Victoria via the Quarry line. 7798 was one of the 12 units temporarily converted to '4VEG'.

Below:
Kearsney May 1985: Originally named 'Ewell', the station opened in 1862, a year later than the line itself from Canterbury to Dover. A memory of its original identity survives in the faded station title painted on the brickwork seen here. '4CEP' No 1559 heads a service from Victoria towards Dover.

Above right:
Kemsing May 1985: A Southern Railway concrete footbridge frames '4VEP' No 7868, operating from Margate, via Canterbury West, to Victoria. The station opened with the line from Otford Junction to Maidstone in 1874.

Right:
Knockholt July 1982: '4CEP' No 1589 is paired with a '4VEP' unit on a boat train service from Victoria to Dover, via Herne Hill. The scene pre-dates the opening of the M25 motorway, which now crosses the railway at this point. Knockholt received a station in 1876, eight years after the opening of the line between Chislehurst and Tonbridge.

Right:

Knockholt July 1982: DMLV No 68006 leads a boat train formation towards the station, en route from Folkestone Harbour to Victoria via Herne Hill. Upon opening, the station had been named 'Halstead for Knockholt'.

Below:

Lancing July 1969: 'ED' No E6008 passes Lancing with a long train of four-wheeled vans, an unidentified working. Lancing station had not, at this time, been rebuilt to its present appearance. No E6008 was later renumbered 73102 and carried the name *Airtour Suisse*. It was renumbered again to become 73212, during its time with Gatwick Express. In more recent times, it was transferred to Network Rail, when an all-over yellow livery was applied.

Bottom:

Leatherhead June 1979: '4EPB' No 5108 on a Waterloo-Effingham Junction service, enters the station, past the rather shabby signalbox. The first station at Leatherhead, dating from 1859, was operated jointly by the LSWR and the LBSCR. In 1867, the LBSCR built its own station, which is the one the '4EPB' is approaching. A separate LSWR station also opened in 1867, to the west of this station, but was closed by the Southern Railway in 1927. From that date, all services used the surviving LBSCR station, electrification having arrived in 1925.

Above:

Lenham May 1985: Characteristically deep, rectilinear LCDR awnings are in evidence here, framed by a Southern Railway concrete footbridge. The station buildings date from the opening of the line to Ashford in 1884, although they do not feature the cream coloured brickwork found at certain other stations along the route. '4CEP' No 1537 is departing on a Victoria service from Ashford.

Left:

Lewes April 1968: The station hosts '4CIG' No 7334, heading a Victoria to Eastbourne, Hastings and Ore service. The line from Brighton opened in June 1846, while that from Keymer Junction followed just 16 months later.

Above left:

London Bridge March 1982: Standard BR '4EPB' No 5306 has just come round the curve from Borough Market Junction on a service from Charing Cross to Gravesend, via Bexleyheath. One of the towers at Cannon Street, about half a mile away, appears above the second vehicle. The high-level platforms at London Bridge date from 1864, when the line was extended to reach Charing Cross. Cannon Street opened two years later, in 1866.

Left:

London Bridge June 1981: '4BEP' No 7014 waits under the overall roof with a stopping service to Brighton. Services over the route that No 7014 is about to use had commenced in June 1839 but Brighton itself was not reached until 1841.

Top:

London Bridge May 1982: '4VEP' No 7857 heads an eight-coach formation through Platform 5, on a service from Charing Cross to Margate, via Dover. The then quite new footbridge is already beginning to fit comfortably into the scene.

Right:

Lymington Junction April 1986: '2HAP' No 6090 speeds round the bend from Brockenhurst towards the junction site, displaying the headcode for a semi-fast service from Waterloo to Bournemouth, perhaps providing somewhat limited accommodation.

Left:
Maidstone Barracks March 1983: The ex-LCDR main line from Swanley to Maidstone East crosses over the former SER Medway Valley line at this point. '4EPB' No 5232 is *en route* from Strood to Maidstone West, a line electrified in 1939. This line was opened in 1856, the onward route to Paddock Wood having opened 12 years earlier, in 1844.

Bottom left:
Martello Tunnel April 1984: '4CEP' No 1527 leaves the 533-yard tunnel, en route to Margate heading a train from Charing Cross.

Top right:
Merstham August 1979: The station, with its signalbox behind a concrete barrier, greets '4CIG' No 7399 on a Brighton service. In the background is the Quarry line, bypassing Merstham and Redhill. The M25 motorway is crossed here by both lines.

Centre right:
Minster May 1986: An exposed spot at the western point of a triangle, with lines radiating to Ashford, Ramsgate and Dover. Against a misty background, 'Jaffa Cake'-liveried '4CEP' No 1515 arrives on a Margate to Charing Cross service, via Canterbury West. An imposing signalbox overlooks the Ramsgate line, also the loop of 1929, leading to Minster South Junction and Dover. The station was built in 1846 when the line from Ashford to Ramsgate Town opened.

Below:
Mitcham Junction October 1975: The signalbox witnesses the passage of '2EPB' No 5651, en route from Wimbledon to West Croydon. Croydon Tramlink now uses the route, flying over the line to Sutton at this point.

for the Modeller and Historian

Right:

Mountfield April 1986: Caught in the weeks leading up to the replacement of the Hastings diesel units by EMUs is '4CEP' No 1522, on a trial run. It is travelling south, between Robertsbridge and Battle, not far from Mountfield and has been out-shopped in 'Jaffa Cake' livery.

Below:

New Malden August 1979: The island platform had been out of service for many years at this time, suburban services using only the outer platform faces on the slow lines. '4SUB' No 4656 visits the station on a Shepperton service. Malden had been rebuilt during 1934-35 and was renamed New Malden in the 1950s.

Bottom:

Norwood Junction April 1983: '4CIG' No 7438, the final member of the class, leads a 12-coach train through the station, on the original 1839 route from London Bridge. It is en route to Littlehampton via the Quarry line and Hove. Norwood Junction had begun life as 'Jolly Sailor', on a nearby site.

Above:

Norwood Junction April 1983: The signalbox as viewed from the station, with '4VEP' No 7804 bringing an eight-coach formation from Coulsdon North to London Bridge, via Tulse Hill.

Below:

Orpington March 1981: 'ED' No 73108 brings an assortment of vehicles through Platform 2, the headcode implying an operation within the broadest limits of Margate and Bricklayer's Arms, via Deal. No 73108 started life numbered E6014 and was scrapped in 2004.

Below:

Orpington March 1981: Recently refurbished at Swindon, '4CEP' No 411514 leads a boat train through Platform 3. Bound for Dover, it had come via Herne Hill. The use of a TOPS six-character identity was a brief fashion for these units. The station buildings date from 1901 and replaced those of 1868, contemporary with the opening of the line from Chislehurst to Tonbridge, the 'Sevenoaks cut-off'. The EMU depot roof is glimpsed behind the signalbox.

Bottom:

Paddock Wood August 1974: The down side canopy echoes the characteristics of that on the up side. A bay platform serves the needs of Medway Valley line services to Maidstone West and Strood. While '4VEP' No 7866 stands in the down through platform on a train to Margate via Dover, '2HAP' No 6153 waits in the bay, with a Medway Valley train.

Right:

Paddock Wood March 1983: The simple station building, with canopy, on the up side hosts '4CEP' No 7205, one of the final batch of units in the class. It is operating a train from Margate to Charing Cross, via Canterbury West.

Bottom right:

Penge East March 1981: Taken from the cab of '4EPB' No 5351, '4CEP' No 7116 enters the station, having just emerged from the 1 mile 381 yard Penge Tunnel. It is leading an eight-coach formation on a Ramsgate via Chatham service from Victoria.

Far left:
Petersfield May 1982: With the trackbed of the former Midhurst branch to the right, '4CIG' No 7344 brings a Portsmouth Harbour semi-fast service into the station from Waterloo.

Left:
Petersfield April 1984: '4VEP' No 7840 crosses the main road, with a stopping service from Waterloo to Portsmouth & Southsea. The substantial signalbox, controlling the crossing, survives at the time of writing. Midhurst branch services used to depart from a separate platform, north of the crossing, the site of which is here obscured by the '4VEP'. However, evidence of the former branch is provided by the second arch to the bridge in the background.

Bottom left:
Petts Wood March 1982: '4EPB' No 5151 enters the station, opened in 1928, with an Orpington to Charing Cross service.

Right:
Pirbright September 1986: Unpowered '4TC' No 419 heads a Bournemouth semi-fast service, propelled by a '4REP' tractor unit. The location is near to the junction where the Aldershot and Alton line diverges to the south.

Below:
Pluckley May 1986: Staggered platforms are a feature of SER-built stations, this being no exception. '4VEP' No 7838 passes through on a Margate via Dover to Charing Cross service. The original wooden buildings on the down side form a backdrop and it is highly probable these date from 1842, when the line opened.

Left:
Polhill Tunnel July 1980: This well-known setting finds one of the final batch of '4CEP' units, No 7208, racing downhill on an eight-coach train towards Dunton Green and Sevenoaks, on a Charing Cross to Margate via Dover service. When new, No 7208 had operated, albeit briefly, 'rush hour' services between Waterloo and Portsmouth.

Below:
Portcreek Junction June 1978: '2HAP' No 6053 leads a '4VEP' unit on a semi-fast service from Brighton to Portsmouth Harbour. By the time this picture was taken, the A27 road overbridge had been built, altering the backdrop. Furthermore, the former junction signalbox had been removed, as surplus to requirements, following an area re-signalling scheme.

Right:
Portcreek Junction March 1989: '4CIG' No 1246 leads a 12-coach train over Portcreek, en route to Waterloo from Portsmouth Harbour. The leading unit is in the original NSE styling, with a paler shade of blue than that used later, with angled lining beneath the cab window.

Below right:
Portsmouth & Southsea August 1982: A batch of 12 '4VEP' units (7788-99) had been remodelled internally for Gatwick services, with increased luggage accommodation and reclassified as '4VEG' (7901-12), yet they frequently found use elsewhere and here is one of the 12 units, No 7904, operating from Portsmouth Harbour to Victoria. This sub-class was later disbanded, the units regaining their original identities.

Above:
Portsmouth & Southsea July 1988: On a day when No 73130 was named *City of Portsmouth*, the Class 73 descends from the high level, with a '4CIG' in tow. The high-level rebuilding had then recently been completed. In the sidings, the difference between the two styles of NSE lining is clearly evident, the sharp angle, as seen on the left, being superseded by the curved effect, seen to the right. On this day, a 'Deltic' and a 'Class 37' also visited the station as exhibits. Originally numbered E6037, 73130 later lost its name when adapted for use by Eurostar, acquiring a grey livery.

Below:
Preston Park May 1978: '4CIG' No 7335, the penultimate Phase I unit, approaches the Cliftonville spur junction, with a fast train to Victoria. Suburban stock dating from 1925, in departmental use as unit No 014, stands alongside the former Pullman Car workshop. Such 'de-icing' units had been reduced to two-car formation, with the two intermediate trailer vehicles removed.

Above:

Preston Park July 1983: '4BEP' No 7022, the final member of its class, leads a semi-fast Quarry line train from Victoria to Brighton past the up carriage sidings, situated just to the north of Preston Park station.

Left:

Ramsgate August 1974: The station is host to BR(SR) '4EPB' No 5302, about to depart for Victoria, via Canterbury West and Maidstone East. A rake of '2HAP' units is parked in No 1 lay by, with No 6070 displaying the Chatham route code 50. The original pre-1926 SER Ramsgate Town, terminus station, was to the right of the line of '2HAPs'.

Below:

Ramsgate January 1983: '4CEP' No 7147 waits to leave from Platform 4 for Victoria, via Chatham, at the Margate end of the station. In the background is the EMU maintenance depot, where the steam motive power depot had once stood.

Above left:
Raynes Park December 1983: '4VEP' No 7716 charges down the fast line with a Basingstoke service from Waterloo. The signalbox here, since demolished, never seemed quite vertical, although this was probably an optical illusion. The 1859 Epsom branch diverges at this point, the down track seen in the foreground, with the points set for Motspur Park.

Left:
Selhurst September 1975: The station, dating from 1865, bathed in low autumn sunshine, finds '4SUB' No 4738 calling on a Victoria service from West Croydon. The overhead electrification from Balham to Coulsdon North lasted for just four years, from 1925.

Top:
Selling May 1986: 'Jaffa Cake'-liveried '4CEP' No 1595 passes the signalbox on the up platform, with a train from Dover Western Docks to Victoria.

Centre right:
Selling May 1986: '4CEP' No 1566 arrives on a Faversham to Dover service, coupled to a DMLV unit. Selling station opened with the line from Faversham to Canterbury East in 1860. New lighting poles are in position, soon to replace the Southern Railway concrete lamp standards.

Right:
Sevenoaks August 1979: '4EPB' No 5136 waits in Platform 4a on a service to Holborn Viaduct. Meanwhile, '6L' DEMU No 1013 pounds through Platform 2 on an up Cannon Street train from Hastings.

Left:
Shawford May 1988: A pair of Class 73 electro-diesel locomotives powers a Waterloo semi-fast service from Bournemouth, during the months when almost anything could happen; a time when the '4REP' units were being withdrawn for their electrical equipment to be refurbished for use in new Class 442 units.

Below:
Sheerness-on-Sea August 1979: The terminus, two platforms and a centre track, is visited by '2HAP' No 6113 on the shuttle service from Sittingbourne. The line to Sheerness opened in 1860, two years after the Sittingbourne main line.

Right:
Shepperton August 1979: Scarcely a terminus in style, the station had been built with continuation to Chertsey in mind. The LSWR gained ownership of the line in 1864, at which time there had been murmurings of interest by the GWR. In this view, '4SUB' No 4656 waits to return to Waterloo, via Kingston, a service electrified since 1916.

Bottom right:
Shortlands March 1981: The prototype for the refurbishment of the '4CEP' family of units was unit No 7153, distinguishable from the production series inasmuch as it never received hopper ventilators. It is approaching the station, heading a 12-coach boat train from Victoria to Folkestone Harbour, via Herne Hill. The brake van sections in each outer vehicle were replaced by passenger accommodation, with the brake van section transferred to an internal vehicle. The middle unit in this picture is unrefurbished, retaining brake vans in the outer vehicles, while the rear unit is an example from the Swindon refurbishment series, with hopper ventilators and revised accommodation.

Right:
St May Cray February 1981: '4CEP' No 7175 is en route to Victoria, having travelled from Margate, via Canterbury West and Maidstone East. The station was rebuilt in the late 1950s, when electrification was extended beyond Gillingham and Maidstone East, to serve the main lines to east Kent. Quadruple track extends from Shortlands Junction through to Swanley Junction, where the Maidstone and Rochester lines diverge.

Above:
Strawberry Hill August 1979: The depot hosts two stored '4CEP' units, No 7149 and No 7204 (which reveals evidence of a severe fire).

Left:
Streatham Hill August 1979: '4SUB' No 4695, equipped with roller blinds, heads a service from Victoria to Beckenham Junction. Streatham Hill depot sidings, in the background, occupy both sides of the line, with a covered shed on the up side.

Above:

Surbiton August 1979: Services to Hampton Court traditionally use the outer face of the down island platform; '4SUB' No 4639 enters Platform 4 on one such service. The trackwork at Surbiton had been extensively remodelled in the late 1930s, when the station was the focus of a major rebuilding scheme.

Left:

Sutton July 1985: Climbing past the 'Wall of Death' is refreshed '4EPB' No 5405 heading an eight-coach train. The Southern Railway built the line connecting Sutton with Wimbledon in 1929/30, electrified from its inception. Train services along the line were out-and-back from/to London, serving London Bridge and Victoria.

Below:
Swanley February 1981: A pair of '2HAP' units, with No 6130 leading, approaches on a semi-fast service from Ramsgate to Victoria via Herne Hill. One of the Southern Railway's distinctive signalboxes stands just west of the junction, where the lines to Rochester and Maidstone East go their separate ways.

Bottom:
Swanley February 1981: Refurbished '4CEP' No 411514 brings a Ramsgate to Victoria train through Platform 1, routed via Herne Hill.

SOUTHERN EMUs BEFORE PRIVATISATION

Right:

Sway April 1986: One of the original batch of 20 '4VEP' units, No 7709, departs with a stopping train from Bournemouth to Waterloo. The line from Lymington Junction to Christchurch opened in 1888, this event dating Sway station.

Below:

Sydenham June 1983: The Crystal Palace line diverges from the London Bridge to Norwood Junction main line at this point and the movement of empty stock to and from Streatham Hill depot makes use of this route. The rake of '4CIG' units, led by No 7313, forms one such movement, the route code suggesting a service from Brighton to London Bridge, via the Quarry line. It is about to be overtaken by an up Caterham train. The left fork takes the flyover, the route to Crystal Palace.

Above:

Tonbridge June 1982: '4CEP' No 7186 waits at Platform 3 on a stopping service from Charing Cross to Ashford. The SER main line to Tonbridge, via Redhill, opened in 1842, the Sevenoaks 'cut-off' of 1868 shortening the journey by more than 12 miles. The station buildings, as seen here, are of Southern Railway design, featuring Crittall-style windows.

Below:

Tonbridge August 1982: The approach from Ashford meets the line from Tunbridge Wells at the junction. '4CEP' No 1591 is about to call at the station on a stopping service from Ashford to Charing Cross. The steam motive power depot once stood in the fork of these lines. A '4EPB' is seen parked alongside the up Hastings line.

Left:

Tulse Hill September 1975: '4EPB' No 5018 has just emerged from the 331-yard Knights Hill Tunnel, on a London Bridge 'circular' and is about to enter the station. The Tulse Hill to Herne Hill spur, dating from 1869, is seen to the left.

Left:

Tulse Hill August 1979: An eight-coach train of 'CIG' stock, with No 7335 leading the way, comes round the bend from Herne Hill. The train, allegedly bound for Brighton, via Crystal Palace, should have come from London Bridge, via the right-hand set of lines in the background. Evidently, on this occasion, there were diversions and it is possible the train began its journey at Blackfriars. Tulse Hill opened in 1868 with the LBSCR's 'Portsmouth line' from London Bridge.

Below:

Twickenham August 1979: An expanse of platform space greets '4EPB' No 5115 on a service from Waterloo to Windsor, via Richmond. The station dates from rebuilding in 1954, when the 1848 original was replaced. Large crowds use the station on days when rugby matches are played nearby.

Above left:
Vauxhall May 1982: Class 508 No 508012 arrives on a service from Waterloo to Hampton Court. Vauxhall had opened in 1848 along with Waterloo, its title subsequently shortened from the inaugural 'Vauxhall Bridge'.

Left:
Victoria March 1982: The LCDR terminus finds '4CEP' No 7134 waiting in Platform 4, about to go to Margate via Maidstone East and Canterbury West. The station was opened in 1862, following the construction of Grosvenor Bridge across the River Thames.

Top:
Victoria May 1982: '4CEP' No 1523 is departing from Platform 5, on a Ramsgate train via the Catford loop. The LBSCR terminus, situated alongside, had opened two years earlier, in 1860.

Right:
Wandsworth Common May 1982: '4BEP' No 7019 threads its way through the cutting from Clapham Junction, en route from Victoria to Eastbourne, Hastings and Ore. The original station had opened in 1856 on a different site.

Above:
Wandsworth Common May 1982: The station curve is accentuated by the effect of the telescopic lens. '4CIG' No 7394 brings a semi-fast Brighton to Victoria service, via the Quarry line, through Platform 4. The present station, built in 1869, replaced the original structure.

Right:
Waterloo March 1982: Platform 2 finds No 508003 about to depart on a nocturnal service to Chessington South. The Class 508s lasted in service on the Southern for only about four years. Then, in three-car form, they were exiled to Merseyside, at a time when Class 455s were being delivered to the Southern Region and third rail electrification was being extended on Merseyside.

Right:

Waterloo East August 1979: A view taken from a temporary footbridge, affording an unusual study of the canopy roof. At Platform C is a service to Margate, via Dover, with '4CEP' No 7177 leading the way.

Below:

Waterloo East February 1981: Platform C finds '4EPB' No 5156 en route from Charing Cross to Gravesend, via Bexleyheath. Until 1911, there had been a line connecting this station with the LSWR terminus, across the road.

Bottom:

Waterloo East March 1985: Two '4EPB' units enter the station together, on Platforms B (No 5049 left, from Hayes) and D (No 5200 right, from Orpington).

Left:
West Croydon March 1983: A cluttered scene at the London end of the station, as refreshed '4EPB' No 5442 enters on a Sutton and Epsom Downs service. The signalbox is perched high on a gantry, while semaphores still control movements.

Centre left:
West Norwood Junction July 1985: The sinuous route from Tulse Hill is depicted here, as refreshed '4EPB' No 5431 rises to meet the line from Streatham Hill. The train from London Bridge is bound for East Croydon.

Below:
West Worthing February 1984: This had been the western extremity of the main line electrification scheme of 1933. The carriage shed seen here, was built by the Southern Railway and survived in a state of dereliction for many years after becoming redundant. Later, its future seemed assured, when clearance of vegetation and, presumably, re-energising of the third rail took place. However, plans changed and the shed has been demolished. A rake of '4CIG' units is parked on the outside siding, while '4CAP' No 3201 passes on a service to Littlehampton.

Above:

Weybridge June 1984: The line to Chertsey had opened in 1848, the continuation to Virginia Water following in 1866, with electrification dating from 1937. A service from Weybridge takes the Chertsey line, with ex-Tyneside '2EPB' No 5782.

Below:

Wimbledon July 1988: Two units in NSE livery sandwich a '4VEP' in BR blue/grey. Leading '4CIG' No 1815 carries its identity beneath the grab rail, an absurd idea that did not last long. No 1815 was later raised to 'Greyhound' status, and renumbered 1302. This 12-coach train, bound for Bournemouth on a stopping service, is passing the newer of the two EMU stabling points at Wimbledon, which stands on ground previously occupied by Durnsford Road Power Station.

Above:

Wimbledon July 1988: Empty stock leaves the depot to join the up fast line at Wimbledon Staff Halt. The formation comprises two '4VEP' units, with NSE-liveried No 3004 leading. Code 53 suggests, erroneously, it is a service from Alton.

Right:

Wimbledon July 1988: Low evening sun catches 'ED' No 73119 on a semi-fast service from Bournemouth to Waterloo, during the transition period, when Class 442 units were coming into service and '4REPs' were being decommissioned. No 73119, here bearing the name *Kentish Mercury*, had originally carried the identity E6025. The locomotive was renamed *Borough of Eastleigh* in 2009.

Above:
Wimbledon July 1988: A stopping train to Bournemouth passes the former goods yard, a site already in alterative use. It is a 10-coach formation with a '2HAP' carrying its final identity, No 4313, ahead of two '4VEP' units.

Below:
Winchester April 1985: '4REP' No 3009 is in charge of a Waterloo semi-fast from Bournemouth. The land to the right was the site of Winchester goods yard.

Above:
Windsor & Eton August 1979: With an inspection saloon in tow, 'ED'
No 73102 waits in the station, shortly to propel the former LMS vehicle
back towards Staines. The terminus opened in 1849. (See the caption for
Lancing for details of No 73102.)

Below:
Woking May 1967: Steam services have just two months to go as 'ED'
No E6012 brings an up Southampton boat train towards St John's cutting.
A '4TC' set leads the formation, with a buffet car replacing the TFK.
No E6012 was later renumbered 73106 and was scrapped in 2004.

Above:

Woking June 1986: '4CIG' No 7343 is leaving Platform 4 on a stopping train to Portsmouth Harbour, while '2HAP' No 6078 stands alongside in bay Platform 5. The imposing Southern Railway signalbox towers over the scene. Platforms 4 and 5 later became 5 and 6 when the island platform bay was inserted.

Right:

Woking May 1988: 'ED' No 73005 is in charge of an Alton special, the 'Watercress Belle', on the occasion of a rail show in the down goods yard. No 73005 had been one of the original six locomotives of the class, carrying the identity E6005. It was later named *Mid Hants Watercress Line* and is now preserved on the Severn Valley Railway.

Below:

Worplesdon September 1986: Shabby station canopies frame the arrival of '4CIG' No 7415 on a stopping service from Waterloo to Portsmouth Harbour. The station dates from 1883, 38 years after the line from Woking to Guildford opened.

Above:
Bickley Junction September 1999: Eurostar services started in 1994, just prior to the Privatisation of British Rail. Seen after nearly five years in service, yet unchanged in appearance, a formation approaches the junction, having travelled from Waterloo International via the Waterloo Curve viaduct. It is about to take the Tonbridge Loop to Petts Wood Junction.

Left:
Brockenhurst August 1988: Rounding the curve smoothly, on its way from Waterloo to Bournemouth, is Class 442 No 2411 in original condition. Doors concealing jumper cable gear are in place, but later, this was not always the case.

Top right:
Fratton August 1991: Lines of brand-new Class 456 units are seen stored in the former goods yard, awaiting modifications prior to entry into service. This work was undertaken by Fratton EMU depot. The area seen here is now largely a retail park.

Right:
St Mary Cray Junction April 1999: Class 465 'Networkers' entered service during the early 1990s, bearing Network SouthEast livery. One such unit, No 465045, is seen approaching the junction in original form, shortly after Privatisation.

Above:
Surbiton July 1988: Almost brand-new, two Class 442 units form a 10-car train from Waterloo to Weymouth, to which terminus only the leading unit will travel onwards from Bournemouth. The jumper cable covers are in place.

Below:
Wimbledon July 1988: Class 319 No 319006, fresh into service, drifts past the down yard on an anti-clockwise service from Blackfriars, down via Tooting and back via Sutton. The goods yard, already reduced in scale, was to close shortly.